I0473861

HOME-BASED BUSINESS IDEAS

10 Easy to Start Businesses You Can
Operate From Home
Without Being Internet Savvy!

By S. Williams

Table Of Content

INTRODUCTION

On the next few pages, you will find ten low start-up business outlines. We will discuss estimated start up costs, as well as, provide suggestions on how to best market that particular venture. Whenever possible, names and addresses of where to obtain further information or products will be provided (note: the names and addresses if offered are done so without any guarantees regarding the vendors).

It took months to put this information together and by purchasing this book, you have save yourself a great deal of time and money. As you read each business outline, you should be able to determine if it is for you or not.

The businesses outlines in this book are low start-ups because they can be started for less than two thousand dollars in most cases. One of the best things about these businesses is that they do not require any special skills and you can get started relatively quickly.

Our goal was to make the information simple yet as complete as possible. We wanted to make it possible, for you the reader, to put down this book and get started. The outlines are starting points and a more detailed business plan would be a plus.

Please keep in mind that success is not guaranteed. These outlines are not blueprint to success, but rather suggestions on how to implement a particular business. The success you achieve will depend on your commitment, ability and some good fortune from heaven. Good fortune is included because timing is very, very, important. If you start the right business at the right time, the possibilities are endless.

Read each outline carefully, being sure to write notes for yourself as to your likes and dislikes for a particular venture. Once you have chosen those you like best, go over them and choose the business for you.

No matter what business you chose, you will most likely need a business license. Therefore check with your local County & State licensing agencies to determine what licenses if any are needed.

With the business for you decided, it is time for you to begin. **Start today!!! Don't wait!! Your financial future is in your hands!!!!!**

ANSWERING SERVICE

START-UP COST: $300

MARKETING PLAN: Classified Ads, Fliers and Business cards, Website

EQUIPMENT: Extra Phone Lines, Office Supplies (pens, message pads, bin to place messages labels and labeler to label bins)

POSSIBLE VENDORS: Local Phone Company and Office Supply Store

There are many businesses and busy professionals who need and currently use answering service or offices assistances. If you don't mind your phone ringing constantly, then this might be the business for you.

Depending on how many lines you have and the type of phone you use, your start up cost could increase. The estimated cost above is for one extra line, call waiting, an inexpensive single line phone and your miscellaneous office supplies.

The main purpose of a marketing plan is to let people know of your existence. The suggestions given above are by no means engraved in stone. If you have others ideas you prefer and have proven to be successful for you, please don't hesitate to use them.

I am often amazed at how many people read classified ads. What's great about these types of ads is that they do not cost much to place. You could put an ad in your local paper offering your services. Remember, stress the level of professionalism you can and will provide.

To supplement your classified ad, you may also want to create a flier to distribute along with your business card to potential customers. Your flier should be more of a fact sheet listing your services, prices and any special deals you might offer to entice your potential customer to become a paying client.

Developing a good website is probably the best thing you can do for your business. On every printed ad you distribute, should contain your web address for them to visit to get more detailed information about your business. Your website will work for you 24/7 if promoted correctly. Try searching for free websites, which will keep your start-up costs low. The site will most likely be a web page but depending on how much you want to use it in your business, a page will be fine to direct people for more information.

For the sake of order, we suggest you use a separate bin to store messages for each of your clients. As each of your client's calls is forwarded to you, take the message and place it in the appropriate bin. When your client calls in for messages, you'll retrieve the messages in the bin with their name.

CAR WASH/DETAILING

START-UP COST
Under $500 Depending on How Elaborate You Want to Start

MARKETING PLAN
Fliers, Word of Mouth, Coupons, Business Cards, Car Magnet on Your Car

EQUIPMENT
Bucket, Sponges, Cleaning Solution, Car Wax, Rags, Garden Hose, Cordless Vacuum, Water Tank (to Offer Mobile Service-start up may increase depending on size of tank)

POSSIBLE VENDOR
Automotive Store, Office Supply Store, eBay

This is a great business for young adults, as well as, the whole family to be involved in to make some extra money. This is the type of business, which will always have customers because every car owner is a potential customer.

A hand car washing business is probably one of the easiest businesses to start. With a cordless vacuum cleaner, you can provide that extra professional touch.

Some people charge, $25.00 to hand wash and wax a car and about $7.00 for just a plain wash. If two or three people work on a car, it will be done in no time. When pricing your service, don't forget to check the area to see what the competition (automated car washes) is charging.

Offering a mobile car washing/ detailing service can greatly increase your customer base. You can distribute your fliers, coupons, and business cards at local office complexes offering to wash their cars while they work. Most car owners love their cars and want only the best, therefore stress the care you take to do a great job.

CHEF FOR HIRE

START-UP COST
Under $550 Depending on the Quality of
Your Equipment

MARKETING PLAN
Flier, Business Card, Ad in Local Paper,
Word of Mouth, Website, Mailing list of Target
Market

EQUIPMENT
Food Processor, Quality Pots and Pans, Misc.
Kitchen Utensils, Cookbooks

POSSIBLE VENDOR
Department Store Household Dept.,
Restaurant Supply Store, eBay

In today's busy society, people are having less and less time to prepare a home cooked meal and even less time to try out exotic recipes. If you like to cook, you could fill this need for those individuals who don't have time or just don't want to cook meals.

Preparing healthy meals with lots of flavor is a skill, which is in great demand. More and more individuals are living a healthy lifestyle and would appreciate healthy meals that taste great.

You may want to offer both in home preparation and also delivery service. You are a chef for hire who will prepare a meal, right in their own home or deliver it to them. If you prepare the meal in their home, you may want to uses their equipment in the beginning, but having your own is always best.

Develop your website, make some fliers, attach a business card and mail to your target market, place ads in you local paper, tell your friends and you are on your way. Don't forget to check your local licensing bureau to determine if any special permits are needed.

BONN APPETITE !!!

DJ SERVICE

START-UP
$1,500

MARKETING PLAN
**Website, Business Cards, Other Vendors
(i.e. Wedding Planner, Events Planner, and
Caterer, just to name a few), Car Magnet**

EQUIPMENT
**Disc Player or MP3 Player, Speakers,
Spot Lights, Strobe Light (Optional for Atmosphere),
Your Favorite Music.**

POSSIBLE VENDOR
**Audio Store, Electronic Store, Flea Market,
Yard Sale, eBay**

With good music and a good sound system, you could make some good money nightly as a DJ. It doesn't hurt to have a gimmick. You want people to remember you. You want to be in demand.

Networking with other vendors in the entertainment field can be a great source of referral business. Your goal is to have a caterer, or events planner call you when they are hired for job.

The quality of your equipment is important. You might consider checking out flea markets, yard sales, and swap meets to purchase some quality used equipment. Your music should be sought after.

Probably the biggest challenge of this business is keeping it from being seasonal. By seasonal I mean, you don't want to be employed just during wedding season, the holiday season and graduation season. You want to be the DJ people think of when they are giving birthday parties, anniversary parties, and any other type of celebration.

The music you deliver is important, but equally important is professionalism. You need to be dependable. Arrive early and give more than you promised.

A well designed website can be a great marketing tool used to detail your business. If possible, a sample of the type of music you offer and your mixing skills would be a plus. Your website is your chance to show case your talents.

Car magnets are another great tool. They can be used to direct people to your website, as well as, tell people about your business as they are stopped at a traffic light, waiting in traffic, or parked on the street. Like a website, the magnets are constantly working for you.

As always, when determining price, check out your competition.

INTERIOR HOUSE PAINTING

START-UP COST
$1,000

MARKETING PLAN
Fliers, Business Cards, Classified Ads, Website, Car Magnet, Referrals

EQUIPMENT
Brushes, Motorized Painting Tools, Ladder, Drop Cloth, Tape, Paint Tray, Misc. Items

POSSIBLE VENDOR
Hardware Store, eBay

This would be a great business for a group of young friends. Whether in high school or college a group of three to four friends could start this business and they can hire there friends if they need extra help.

This would also make a great family business because this is the type of business everyone can participate in. The kids could hand out the fliers as well as paint areas, which are not dangerous, depending on their age.

Quality service and on time completion should be your main selling points. You could charge your client by the room or by the square footage. Once again, my advice to you is to do your homework and check out your competition to see what they are doing.

Before and after you have completed a job, don't forget to take pictures. You want to develop a portfolio of your work to show potential clients in the future.

Let people know you are in business by creating a flier offering some kind of discount. Mail or deliver these fliers to your potential customers. Placing a classified ad in the "for hire" section of your local paper is another way to let people know you are in business.

Again website and car magnets are other useful advertising tools you can use to try and gain new customers. No matter what form of advertising you use, you should always offer to give a free estimate. The word "free" is very powerful and you should use it as often as you can.

Your overall start-up cost will depend on the quality of the equipment and quantity of equipment you decide to start with.

JANITORIAL/MAID SERVICE

START-UP COST
$800-$1500

MARKETING PLAN
**Business Cards, Car Magnet, Website,
Fliers, Yellow Page Ad, Sales Calls on
Businesses, Referrals**

EQUIPMENT
**Mops, Brooms, Buckets, Sponges, Rags,
Cleaning Solutions, Vacuum Cleaner, Duster,
Polisher, Steam Cleaner, Garbage Bags**

POSSIBLE VENDORS
**Grocery Store, Hardware Store, Department Store,
Office Supply Store**

You probably have most of the items you would need to start in your home. This is another great business for a family to do together and what is also great about this business is that it does not require any special skill level. It does however require a high level of pride in the quality of work you give.

Again, this business would also be great for a group of young people in high school or college to start together.

A person's home is a very special place to them so you must treat it and your customer with respect at all times. This means you do not search through their things, eat their food without permission etc..

Arrive on time, do quality work, leave on time, deliver more than you promised and you should get referral, which is what you, want.

To provide janitorial services to businesses, you introduce them to your business with a flier or a sales call (visit to their establishment) or both. Placing a yellow page ad is another tool you can use to get both commercial and residential customers.

Depending on how much money you have to start, you may want to hire some independent contractors to help you. The more hands available, the more jobs which can be completed. Your ultimate goal should be to one day have a team of people work for you and you just supervise.

When deciding on a price, don't forget to include your labor along with the cost of the products used. Your time is valuable and must be included as a cost of doing business. As always, investigate your competition to see what they are charging.

Always keep in mind that the product you are selling is a service. When selling a service business, deliver of quality service is the key message of all advertising.

JEWELRY DESIGN

START-UP
$500

MARKETING PLAN
**Consignment Store, Mail Order,
Flea Market, Website, Car Magnet**

EQUIPMENT
**Beads, Clasps, Bead Design Board, Wire,
Crimper, Wire Cutter, Storage Case, and Other
Misc. Supplies Depending on What You Are Making**

POSSIBLE VENDOR
Hobby Shop, Craft Shop, Discount Super Store

If you are creative and enjoy working with your hands, this might be the business for you. This is another type of business that is limited only by your imagination. You can designs, bracelets, necklaces, earrings, pins and rings.

Most hobby and craft stores will have everything you need to get started. Once you have gained some experience, you may want to create your own design beads by having them cast. To find a casting company, check the internet.

Your designs are what will distinguish you from the packed so get creative and keep copies of your designs in a book. You may want to consider selling the designs along with the needed materials to make them, as a kit.

Take samples of your work to your local boutiques for them to place orders. Consider creating a catalog of your work being sure to use quality pictures. The catalog can be given to friends and potential customers for them to order from.

Depending on your artistic abilities, you may want to offer to create special pieces based on the customer's specification. Custom pieces are great because you can charge more for them.

When pricing your product, do not under estimate the value of your time. The time it takes you to make a piece must be considered along with the cost of the raw materials. Your time is valuable so include it in your price.

Get creative! Begin to look at everyday items with a different eye. Decide who are your customers and design your jewelry to meet their needs.

PARTY PLANNER

STAR-UP COST
$800 or Less

MARKETING PLAN
**Business Cards, Car Magnet, Website,
Referrals, Other Vendors**

EQUIPMENT
Party Supplies, Appointment Book, Mobile Phone

POSSIBLE VENDORS
Party Supply Store, eBay, Office Supply Store

If you are organized and enjoy planning events, this could be the business for you. With a little imagination and a lot of hard work, the possibilities are endless.

Everyone loves a good party and a party with a theme is even better. Start out by developing party ideas that you would like, chances are that others will like them too. Try to come up with unusual yet fun ideas.

The nice thing about this business is that everyone you meet is a potential customer so always give out your business cards.

Your website should have examples of various theme parties. As always make sure your pictures are top quality and clear. Post comments and testimonials from past clients.

Again, please remember this is a service business and as such, the quality of the service you provide is very, very important. As always, promise less and deliver more! Efficiency, creativity and the ability to deliver what you promise should be the main theme of all your advertising.

VIDEOTAPING SERVICE

START-UP COST
$800 or Less Depending on Equipment

MARKETING PLAN
**Website, Business Card, Flier, Car Magnet,
Other Vendors**

EQUIPMENT
**Recording Device and Accessories,
Editing Machine, Tri-Pod, Lights, Carrying Case**

POSSIBLE VENDOR
Camera Store, eBay

If you already own a camcorder or other recording device, then your star-up cost is lower. This is one of the few business outlines we have offered that does require some skill level. Before starting this business, one should be familiar with lighting and editing. Consider taking a class at your local community college's continuing education department to gain the skills you need. Movie making software is available for those interested in using a computer.

One of your best sources of new customer in the beginning may be other vendors such as party planners, DJs, caterers, wedding planner just to name a few. Your business cards should also be unique enough to encourage people to keep it.

When selling your services be sure to impress upon your potential customers that you provide quality work. Referrals from satisfied customers are always the best advertising.

WEDDING CONSULTANT

START-UP COST
$500

MARKETING PLAN
**Business Cards, Other Vendors, Website,
Car Magnet, Local Bridal Shop**

EQUIPMENT
Day Planner, Data Base or File Cabinet

POSSIBLE VENDOR
Office Supply Store, e-Bay, Bridal Shop

Once again good organizational skills are an advantage in this business. Imagination and the ability to listen and remain calm under pressure are also very important.

A good data base contact system is a must. You need to store and be able to retrieve quickly the guest lists of your customers for mailings and responses.

Because this business is so very specialized, placing fliers and business cards in various bridal shops in the area should yield your best results. Give your business cards to other vendors and ask them to give them pass them along when they know of anyone who could use your service.

When dealing with your customers you must develop a rapport. Make your customer feel confident in you. **YOU ARE A RELIABLE PROFESSIONAL!**

On the previous pages, we have presented to you businesses that can be started with relatively little capitol & in many cases you don't need a computer. We have also made suggestions on how to market your business, as well as suggestions on where to find the products needed. As you were reading, you should have been writing down your comments in the space provided and by now you should have an idea which business is right for you.

The businesses suggested were also chosen because no special skill level is need for most of them. Anyone with a desire to become an entrepreneur can do so with one of these businesses without much previous training. They are also good for many different ages. Young adults seeking to become entrepreneurs can also start these businesses.

Deciding which business is for you is step one on your way to achieving your financial goals. Step two involves creating a business plan (which can be purchased from us). This plan would include a marketing program that fits your product, as well as budget. The suggestions we have made through out this report have been low cost and by now means are they your only means of advertising. They were given as a starting point.

Websites were suggested through out this book as a form of advertising. A web page can also be used in many cases. A simple page on the internet which gives details about your business or service is the ultimate goal. If you have a lot of products to offer, a website might be your best bet.

Do your homework to determine which is best for you.

The sources of suppliers we have provided are only a suggested starting point. Do your own homework and locate other sources. Good business sense will tell you that one source for anything is not enough.

Choosing a business entity is also very important. The topic needed to be discussed in detail so we suggest you do investigation or purchase our report "Writing a Business Plan". In it we discuss the pros and cons of various business entities. Most people start as a sole proprietor but the amount of liability you will expose yourself and your family to may dictate the use of another entity.

Starting a business is not easy and no guarantees exist for success. Once you've made your decision to take control of your financial future, *you must act*. Don't analyze your business to death. Your final steps are to make sure you have a sound business plan, to get all the professional advice you need, and to go ahead and start. **You deserve financial security.**

www.ingramcontent.com/pod-product-compliance
Lightning Source LLC
Chambersburg PA
CBHW071603170526
45166CB00004B/1779